THE EMOTIONARY

n. *a dictionary of words that don't exist for feelings that do*

THE EMOTIONARY

n. *a dictionary of words that don't exist for feelings that do*

WORDS BY **EDEN SHER**   COMICS BY **JULIA WERTZ**

RAZORBILL

An Imprint of Penguin Random House
Penguin.com

Text copyright © 2016 Eden Sher
Illustrations copyright © 2016 Julia Wertz

ISBN: 978-1-59514-838-4

Printed in the United States of America

1 3 5 7 9 10 8 6 4 2

DEDICATED TO MY MOTHER, WHO ALWAYS
ENCOURAGED* ME TO USE MY WORDS.

*Forced me against my will

|wuhn| **EMOTIONAL ANARCHY**

|too| **DESPAIR**

|three| **ANNOYING SH*T PEOPLE DO**

|fohr| **NEUTRAL SH*T PEOPLE DO**

|fahyv| **TRAINWRECKONOMICS**

|siks| **RAGE**

|sevuhn| **FOR SHAME**

|eyt| **FLEETING MOMENTS OF HAPPINESS**

Dear Reader,

Feelings—I've had them all. Big ones and small ones and joyful ones and melancholy ones, all of which were urgent and intense, none for which I had words. When I was a little kid, the only way I knew how to communicate was through explosive, nonverbal temper tantrums. But as I got older and screaming became an increasingly less acceptable way of conversing, I knew I had to figure out a way to translate the screaming into less alarming modes of communication.

So off I went on my journey to discover the elusive concept of "rationality." I knew I would understand it eventually. I just needed time.

In fifth grade, after hurling myself into a wall because I realized my hair tie wasn't wrapped exactly four times around my ponytail, I would think "Middle school will be my time!" By the time high school came around, and I was *still* reliant on nonverbal coping mechanisms, I started to lose hope.

At sixteen, I found out I got a 92 on a trigonometry test *and* I was the only girl in the world who hadn't gotten her period yet, so I decided the best course of action was to slam my brand-new laptop into the ground and break the knobs on my dresser. As I was left to weep in the aftermath of my fit of rage, all I could think was, "What is wrong with me? What am I missing? Why am I the only person who doesn't know how to not Feel all the time?" I began to fear I would never learn how to "use my words," and soon that fear became a full-blown Word Phobia, and my **DYSCOMMUNICATIA** (pg. 20) only worsened.

Then I discovered "acting," this insane activity where having extreme feelings was not only accepted, but even encouraged. Though not a complete cure, this at least served as an outlet where I could do all the things I was discouraged from doing in real life (be loud, dramatic, extremely feel-y, etc.). My embarkment on professional emoting was a real turning point in my life. I entered a world in which there were infinite ways to capitalize on my emotional self-indulgence.

But everything shifted when I discovered writing. Writing—the most magical way to be productive with my neuroses, and the eventual cure for my dyscommunicatia. All it took was a bad breakup for me to reach the point of emotional intensity where if I didn't do something constructive, it would destroy me. I saw two options: accept my destiny to be misunderstood and alone forever, or look my phobia in its beady little eyes and rip its wig off. Obviously I chose the latter, which finally allowed me to understand the root of my fear—what if I never found the right words to express the thoughts and feelings in my head? What if there WERE no words? What if I was never understood by anyone ever? This revelation quickly turned into a new obsession: any time I felt a feeling, I immediately and compulsively wrote down all the words I thought it felt like. **THE EMOTIONARY** was born!

Creating a book that exposed to the world my personal inventory of highly irrational feelings felt like the perfect way to combine every hobby, passion, and goal in my life. I somehow figured out a way to work through my deep-seated word phobia and emote in the name of Productivity. I could hide under my blankets and cry all day and claim to be "working." Tissue boxes became a tax write-off!

Even after years of compulsively trying to turn all my feelings into words, I still don't have all the answers. I still suffer from dyscommunicatia. I still have too many feelings and ideas to express to you, and I still live in fear of not having enough words to make you fully understand.[*] I don't expect this to solve any of your problems or make your Feelings any more manageable, but words alleviate confusion, right? And the opposite of confusion is understanding, and understanding facilitates togetherness, and togetherness is the opposite of eternal solitude... right?! I hope you Big-Time Feelers out there will read this and think "NO WAY, I'M NOT THE ONLY ONE WHO FEELS THIS?" And if you relate to some of these words, maybe you'll feel at least a little less crazy! More importantly, maybe *I'll* feel a little less crazy.

Misery loves company, so my goal with **THE EMOTIONARY** is to create the largest, most irrational, anxiety-ridden, miserable community of Big-Time Feelers the world has ever seen.

Or, at the very least, make you grateful you're not me.

Sincerely,
Eden

---

[*] For example, I was asked to write literally five hundred words (fewer words than I usually speak in thirty seconds of conversation) about something *I* created, and instead spent two weeks crying under my coffee table in the fetal position panicking about being a total fraud of a writer.

1
|wuhn|

EMOTIONAL ANARCHY

ILLOGICAL + EMOTE

ILLOGIMOTE

|iˈläjimōt|

v. to feel in a way that contradicts or undermines
one's intellectual understanding (of a situation)

RATIONAL EDEN, WHO DURING DAYLIGHT HOURS SCOFFS AT THE IDEA
OF TEXTING HER EX, IS NO MATCH FOR ILLOGIMOTING EDEN, WHO IS
CRYING ON THE FLOOR AT ONE IN THE MORNING, SCREAMING AT HER EX,
DEMANDING TO KNOW WHY HE IS SET ON DESTROYING HER LIFE.

AMBIVALENCE + DIFFICULTY

AMBIVICULTY

|amˈbivəkəltē|

n. the anxiety of having to make decisions

EMOTE + SPIRAL

EMOTAL

|iˈmōdəl|

v. to feel, think, and judge oneself in rapid
succession, ultimately causing immobility

INABILITY + RELAX

INRELAXABILITY

|ˌinriˈlaksəbilitē|

n. the anxiety of having free time

RE- + COMMEMORATE
REMEMORATE

|riˈmeməˌrāt|

v. to remember something one had been trying not to think about by realizing one had not been thinking about that thing

IMPULSIVE + RATIONAL

IMPULSIONAL

|imˈpəlSH(ə)n(ə)l|

adj. anxious from knowing one is making
a hasty (most likely wrong) decision

RESPONSIBILITY + URGENCY

RESPURGENCY

|riˈspərjənsē|

n. the jolt of anxiety from suddenly remembering something
that one was supposed to do but never did

(EDEN) SHER + PERPLEX
SHERPLEX

|SHe(ə)rˈpleks|

v. to unnecessarily complicate a simple situation

CATASTROPHE + EXTRAPOLATE

CASTRAPOLATE

|kəˈstrapəˌlāt|

v. (of a person or situation) to predict the worst possible outcome based on nonexistent evidence

IRRATIONAL + INDEPENDENT

IRREDEPENDENT

|ˌērədiˈpendənt|

adj. unable to ask for help under any circumstances

15

CONTROL + ANGST

CONTRANGST

|kənˈtrāNG(k)st|

n. the anxiety of not being able to control your
or another's behavior, or a course of events

17

EXPOSURE + PHOBIA

EXPOSOPHOBIA

|eks͵pōzə'fōbēə|

n. the fear of being an active participant of social-networking sites

Submitted by Big-Time
Feeler Stella Topalidou

iPHONE + PARANOIA

iPHONOIA

|͵īfə'noiə|

n. the suspicion that people are reading one's text messages or emails, or checking one's phone activity over one's shoulder

Should it be a noun?

Perfulsion?

"The inability to stop making changes to something that is FINE?"

PERFECTION + COMPULSIVE

PERFULSIVE

|pərˈfəlsiv|

Maybe shouldn't have its own page?

OR: IMPERFULSIVE?
(IMPERFECT + COMPULSIVE)

adj. unable to accept a "finished" product

OR. ALT:

Thinking of changing this to ASPD

DYSLEXIA, DYSGRAPHIA, ETC.

DYSCOMMUNICATIA

|ˌdiskəmyoōnəˈkāSHə|

n. the inability to articulate a feeling through words

INTENSE + SILENT

INTENSILENT

|inˈtensələnt|

adj. unable to summon a previously formed thought
or opinion due to overpowering emotion

DESPITE THE HOURS I SPENT PRACTICING WHAT I PLANNED
TO SAY IN THE MIRROR, ONCE WE STARTED FIGHTING, I
BECAME COMPLETELY INTENSILENT, AND ALL THAT CAME OUT
WAS "YOU'RE A BUTTHEAD AND I HATE YOU."

PENSIVE + SILENT

PENSILENT

|ˈpensələnt|

adj. too preoccupied thinking about how one is feeling to have the energy to try to articulate it to another

SOMETIMES TOO MANY BRAIN THOUGHTS MAKE IT IMPOSSIBLE TO FORM MOUTH WORDS, RESULTING IN COMPLETE PENSILENCE.

RANT + ANTICIPATION

RANTICIPATION

|ranˌtisəˈpāSHən|

n. anxiety for an impending fight

SKEPTICAL + OPTIMISM

SKEPTIMISM

|ˈskeptəˌmizəm|

n. restrained excitement for something good one anticipates happening

HAPPINESS + APPREHENSIVE

HAPPRIHENSIVE

|hapriˈhensiv|

adj. afraid to pursue what one loves

DEVASTATION + EVADE
DEVADE

|dəˈvād|

v. to purposely avoid asking someone a question, for fear
that they won't give the answer one wants to hear

EGOMANIA + PARANOIA

EGONOIA

|ˌēgəˈnoiə|

n. the belief that people are annoyed by and/or talking about oneself in an unrealistically negative light (often exacerbated by smoking weed)

DISS + MISCONSTRUE

DISSCONSTRUE

|ˌdiskənˈstroō|

v. to misinterpret someone's words as insulting or offensive

Submitted by Big-Time Feeler
Jenny Davis (@jennydrinks)

SOLOPSESS

|säl əp'ses|

v. to harbor emotions about an embarrassing
event that nobody else remembers

DEPART + PHOBIA

DEPARTOPHOBIA

|dəˌpärtəfōbēə|

n. the anxiety of having to say goodbye, especially at a party when one wants to leave

2

|too|

DESPAIR

LOSS + OSTRACIZE

LOSSTRACIZE

|ˈlästrəˌsīz|

v. to reject the support of others in times of grief

33

UNREQUITED + PHOBIA

UNREQUITOPHOBIA

|ˌənriˈkwītəˈfōbēə|

n. the fear of expressing love to someone who may or may not reciprocate

RESPENTFUL

|rəˈspentfəl|

adj. saddened by an inability to feel happy for someone

BEST FRIEND: Guess what? Janie and I are in love!

ME: Oh, cool, great, that's GREAT! I'm so happy for you and I'm *definitely* telling the truth!

...

ME: I LIED!!! I'm not happy for you! I hate you for being happy!

BEST FRIEND: It's okay, I understand. I still love you.

ME: WHAT?! I hate you for understanding! I'm sorry, I'm just overwhelmed with respentment. I hate me for hating you. No, I hate you for not hating me for hating you! I HATE ME FOR HATING YOU FOR NOT HATING ME!

DESPERATION + ISOLATION

DESPOLATION

|ˈdespəlāSHən|

n. the paralysis of wanting to reach out to other people
but being too comfortable in isolation

DISAPPOINTED + APATHY

DISAPATHY

$|\ˌdisˈapəθē|$

n. a state of indifference caused by repeated
past disappointment in people

CONTEMPT + REALIZE

CONTEMPTINIZE

$|kənˈtem(p)təˌnīz|$

v. the disappointment of realizing why a largely disliked person
(for whom one previously had sympathy) is largely disliked

TREPIDATION + SEPARATION

TREPARATION

|ˌtrepərā SHən|

n. preemptive defeat from knowing the time and effort
required to become close with a prospective partner

> AFTER SAM AND I BROKE UP, MY TREPARATION ANXIETY WAS SO
> SEVERE I SCARCELY LEFT MY BED. IT'S NOT THAT I DIDN'T WANT TO DATE
> AGAIN, I JUST WANTED TO SKIP TO THE PART WHERE THEY KNOW MY WHOLE
> LIFE STORY, WE HAVE TONS OF INSIDE JOKES, WE POP EACH OTHER'S
> BACK PIMPLES, AND I CAN FART WITH RECKLESS ABANDON.

DEGRADATION + RELATED

DEGRELATION

|ˌdegrəˈlāSH(ə)n|

n. the process of gradually growing apart from
a relative as one loses common ground

PRODUCTIVE + SEQUESTER
PROQUESTER

|prəˈkwestər|

v. (trans) to obsessively work on a creative endeavor in isolation, neglecting friends, family, and/or other work

LONELINESS + INSANITY
LONESANITY

|lōnˈsanitī|

n. delirium caused by sustained periods of no human company

FAUX + VIBRATION

FAUXBRATION

|fōˈbrāSHən|

n. the phenomenon of feeling your phone vibrate, often out of desperate expectation, when in reality no vibration has occured because no one is trying to contact you and you will in fact probably die alone

REGRET + RETROSPECT

REGRETROSPECT

|riˈgretrəˌspekt|

n. the feeling that if you could do it all over again,
you actually would change all of the things

LOVE + IMPLODE

IMPLOVED

|imˈplōvd|

adj. melancholy from internalizing love

v. **IMPLOVE** |imˈplōv|

VULNERABLE + BARRICADE

VULNERCADE

|ˈvəln(ə)rkād |

n. the barrier surrounding one's heart that
protects one from accepting love

PRE- + LAMENT
PRELAMENT

|ˈprēləˌment|

v. to miss someone before they're gone or something before it has ended

3

|three|

ANNOYING SH*T PEOPLE DO

FEIGN + UNDERSTAND

FEIGNDERSTAND

|ˌfāndərˈstand|

v. to pretend one has finally heard another person after asking them to repeat themselves three plus times

SOLIPSISTIC + PARTICIPATE

SOLISIPATE

|səˈlisəˌpāt|

v. (in conversation) to pretend to listen to another's story while actually completely ignoring it, waiting for one's turn to speak

SELF-FULFILLING + VALIDATE

SELFIDATE

|ˈselfəˌdāt|

v. to go to another for confirmation of
what one already believes to be true

CONTRARIAN + OPINION

CONTROPINION

|ˈkɒntrəpinyən|

n. a distaste for something widely praised, or vice versa

v. **CONTROPINE**

INAPPROPRIATE + CONFIDENT

INAPPIDENT

|inˈapədənt|

adj. having strong convictions regarding something about which one knows very little

THERAPY + -IZE

THERAPIZE

|ˈθerəpīz|

v. to give advice to others based on things one learned in therapy, but never follow the same guidance oneself

DISCREDIT + CONDESCEND

DISCREDISCEND

|disˈkrediˌsend|

v. to share an experience with the intention of making another feel inferior or less enlightened

BRO + OVERWHELM

BROVERWHELM

|ˌbrōvərˈwelm|

v. (trans) to surround with an excess of bros, or overpower with a single bro's bro-ishness

Submitted by Big-
Time Feeler Jessie K.

57

ENTERTAINER + DRAINING

ENTERDRAINER

|ˌen(t)ərˈdrānər|

n. a person who is abrasive or overwhelming in their (often relentless) attempts to amuse others

FOR EXAMPLE, TAKE MY WIFE . . . PLEASE!

INSTAGRAM + INSECURITY

INSTACURITY

|ˌinstəˈkyoorədē|

n. an excessive concern with one's social media presence, influence, and/or likeability

Submitted by Big-Time Feelers Justin Gordon, Samia Khan, and Abdullah Helwani

SELF-CONGRATULATORY + PUN

SELF-PUNGRATULATORY

|self pənˈgrajələˌtôrē|

adj. smug from coming up with an exceptionally good pun

TEXT + INATTENTIVE

INATTEXTIVE

|inəˈtekstiv|

adj. characterized by incessant phone use during social situations

EMPTY + VINDICATE

EMPTICATE

|ˈemptəˌkāt|

v. (trans) to give someone something they wanted after they stop wanting it

EMPTY + CONSOLATION

EMPTOLATION

|ˌemptəˈlāSHən|

n. the useless triumph of finding something one had lost—but now doesn't need

FUTILE + SATISFACTION

FUTIFACTION

|ˌfyoōtiˈfakSHən|

n. the hollow smugness that comes from having been right all along

APOLOGY + INCOMPETENCE

INAPOLOTENCE

|ˌinəˌpälətənts|

n. the inability to admit wrongdoing

LOGIC + PRIORITIZE

LOGITIZE

|ˈläjəˌtīz|

v. to believe logic and rationality are superior to emotion

IR- + RESOLVE

IRRESOLVE

|iˈriˈzälv|

v. to continually bring up an established problem
with no intention of finding a solution

EMOTION + RATIONALIZE

EMOTIONALIZE

|iˈmōSHənəˌlīz|

v. to try to intellectualize one's emotions

IDIOCY + AGGRAVATED

IDIOVATED

|ˈidēəˌvādəd|

adj. frustrated by one's own inability to not be a dumbass

DISTRACTED + LATE

DISTRACTILATE

|diˌstrakˈtəˌlāt|

v. to wake up earlier than expected, use the extra time to be productive, and arrive at one's destination late

TRAFFIC + SNAFU

TRAFU

|traˈfoō|

n. a wrong turn or exit that puts one in bad traffic
or gets one stuck in a construction zone

FAUX + BONUS

FAUXNUS

|ˈfōnəs|

n. an item falsely advertised as free or a favor that is given only with the expectation of one's spending money or returning the favor

NON- + INVITATION

NONVITATION

|ˌnänviˈtāSHən|

n. an insincere and discouraging offer to attend or participate in something

ESOTERIC + ISOLATE

ESOTERILATE

|ˌesəˈterilāt|

v. (in a group) to exclude one or more persons from the conversation by talking about something little known or understood

UNIMPRESSED + DEFLATE

UNIMFLATE

|ənimˈflāt|

v. to disappoint (someone) by not having the reaction
they had hoped to generate in you

adj. **UNIMFLATED** |ənimˈflātd| frustrated by not shocking or
amazing someone with information one assumed would shock or amaze

75

4

|fohr|

NEUTRAL SH*T
PEOPLE DO

EPIPHANY + MAYONNAISE

EPIPHANNAISE

|iˈpifənāz|

n. the moment one realizes aioli and mayonnaise
are exactly the same thing

SNACK + ACTIVITY

SNACKTIVITY

|snakˈtivitē|

n. the act of eating purely for recreation; most likely to occur when bored

MISERABLE + FULL

MISERAFULL

|ˈmiz(ə)rəfəl|

adj. mentally and physically pained from continuing
to eat past the point of being hungry

DEBILITATING INFINITE NEED TO EAT SYNDROME
DINES

|dīnz|

n. the disorder requiring one to compulsively eat food if
it is in front of oneself even when not hungry,
especially when said food is free

RIDICULOUS + REALIZE

RIDICULIZE

|riˈdikyəlīz|

v. to contemplate something that typically goes unquestioned
and realize how bizarre it actually is

DREAM + REALIZE

DREAMALIZE

|ˈdrēm(ə)ˌlīz|

v. to realize the memories one is describing
as factual were actually a dream

TIME + AMNESIA

TIMENESIA

|tīmˈnēZHə|

n. the experience of forgetting the time literally a second after one has checked a clock

NAME + AMNESIA

NAMENESIA

|nāmˈnēZHə|

n. the experience of forgetting someone's name literally one second after they've introduced themselves

CONFUSED + ENLIGHTENMENT
CONFLIGHTENMENT

|kənˈflītnment|

n. the betrayal of learning that something one once thought to be true is not

PARENT + DIFFERENTIATE

DIFPARENTIATE

|ˌdifpəˈrenSHēˌāt|

v. to view one's parent as an objective human in the world

BRILLIANCE + DEBILITATED

DEBRILLITATED

|dəˈbriləˌtātd|

adj. defeated from experiencing genius

v. **DEBRILLITATE** to enervate another with one's brilliance

REPETITION + APATHETIC
REPATHETIC

|ˌrepəˈθetik|

adj. no longer able to distinguish what one thinks about
something due to repeat exposure to said thing[*]

v. REPATHIZE |ˌrepəˈθīz| to see, hear, or read
the same material so many times that one loses
all sight of one's own opinion/instinct

[*]Repathy most commonly occurs in the context of one's own work, typically regarding a
project about which one cares deeply, something requiring multiple edits and revisions (i.e.,
an essay, a screenplay, a painting, a book through which one bares one's soul, etc.)

FLOSS + MASOCHISM

FLOSSICHISM

| ˈfläsəˌkizəm |

n. the unique pleasure/satisfaction one gets
from the pain induced by flossing

SMUDGE + LEFT

SMEDGE

|smej|

n. the (ink, pencil, marker, etc.) blotch appearing on the left
side of one's hand caused by simultaneously writing
and smearing what one has just written*

*Specific to lefthanded people

MELODIC + MONOTONY

MELOTONY

|məˈlätnē|

_n._ the comfort of routine

THE DAILY SIX-CAR PILEUP ON SUNSET HAD BECOME
SO INTEGRAL TO THE MELOTONY OF MY MORNING COMMUTE,
THE CACOPHONY OF BLARING HONKS AND POLICE SIRENS
TOOK ME INSTANTLY TO MY HAPPY PLACE.

DEFEATED + MUTED

DEFUTED

|ˈdəˌfyoōtid|

adj. participating minimally in conversation because the idea of having to explain oneself is too exhausting

PARTIAL + ARTICULATE

PARTICULATE

|pärˈtikyələt|

adj. able to accurately convey only some of one's ideas

NON- + CONVERSATION

NONVERSATION

|ˌnänvərˈsāSHən|

n. a wordless interaction wherein an entire conversation takes place

RESTRAINT + PATIENCE
RESTRAITIENCE

|riˈstrāSHəns|

n. the composure required to listen to someone tell one things one either already knows or strongly disagrees with

STRAINED SYMPATHY
STRYMPATHY

|ˈstrimpəθē|

n. the effortful kindness one gives to well-intentioned annoyers

FLOP + OPTIMISM

FLOPTIMISM

|ˈflaptəˌmizəm|

n. the futile advice one offers for the sake of advice, knowing the recipient's situation will not pan out well in reality

BLAH + CATHARSIS

BLATHARSIS

|bləˈθärsis|

n. the sensation of having a revelatory cathartic moment, only to realize later it did not really mean anything

5

|fahyv|

TRAINWRECKONOMICS

TRAINWRECK + ECONOMICS
TRAINWRECKONOMICS

|trān͵rekəˈnämiks|

n. the study of how and when one shows what a mess
one is in order to get what one wants

IMPERFECTION + EXAGGERATE

IMPERFERATE

|imˈpərfəˌrāt|

v. to overemphasize one's negative qualities with the concealed hope that the person on the receiving end will be scared and run away

EMOTION + ARDUOUS

EMOTUOUS

|iˈmōSHooəs|

adj. requiring (of another person) a lot of patience and acceptance of all one's intense emotions

MIDDLE + DEFICIENT

MIDDEFICIENT

|ˈmidiˌfiSHənt|

adj. incapable of finding an emotional middle ground

RECIPROCATION + APATHETIC
RECIPROTHETIC

|ri͵siprəˈθetik|

adj. feeling indifferent toward someone (for whom one previously had romantic feelings) once they reciprocate affection

SELF + COMPARTMENTALIZE

COMPARTSELFALIZE

|kəmpärt'selfə͵līz|

v. to place value judgment on different parts of oneself

PRAISE + RESISTENT

PRAISISTENT

|prə'zistənt|

adj. unable to take a compliment

PRESSURED + COURTEOUS
PRESSURTEOUS

|prəˈsərtēəs|

adj. behaving in a way that serves others' needs/comfort before one's own

CHUCK CONSTANTLY COMPLAINS ABOUT HIS BOYFRIEND—

HE'S MANIPULATIVE, NEEDY, FINISHES MY CEREAL AND DOESN'T REPLACE IT, HE DOESN'T LIKE *THE SHINING*, AND HE DOESN'T UNDERSTAND PUNS! HE'S CRUSHING MY SOUL!

BUT WHEN I TELL HIM TO STOP BEING SO PRESSURTEOUS AND JUST BREAK UP WITH HIM, HE ALWAYS RESPONDS,

BUT HE'LL BE SO SAD...

ROMANCE + ANGST

ROMANGST

|rōˈmäNG(k)st|

n. the frustration of repeating destructive patterns in one's love life

113

DEVASTATION + RETALIATE

DEVALIATE

|də̩ˈvalē̩ˌāt|

v. to hurt or punish someone (especially in subtle or passive-aggressive ways) in response to their breaking one's heart

INSECURITY + ANTAGONIZE

INSAGONIZE

|insˈagə̩ˌnīz|

v. to behave cruelly to another human due to deep-seated self-loathing

ADRENALINE + CONFLATE

ADRENAFLATE

| əˈdrenəflāt |

v. to mistake intensity for love

DISCREPANCY + INDICATOR

DISCREPICATOR

|disˈkrepəˌkātər|

n. incompatibility red flags

DISAPPOINTMENT + PURSUE

DISPURSUE

|dispərˈsoō|

v. to actively seek out disappointment/failure

DELIBERATE + RELAPSE
DELLAPSE

|dəˈlaps|

v. to understand wholly the consequence of an impulsive decision but choose to do it anyway

EX-PARTNER + MASOCHISM
EXOCHISM

|ˌeksəˈkizəm|

n. the act of torturing oneself by thinking about the existence of an ex

119

MANUFACTURE + ABANDONMENT

ABANUFACTURE

| ə‚bany əfakCHər |

v. to force disappointment onto a romantic partner if they are not, of their own volition, adequately disappointing you

PREEMPT + DESTRUCT

PREDESTRUCT

|ˌprēdəˈstrəkt|

v. to drive away those closest to oneself

SAD + SATISFACTION

SADISFACTION

|ˌsadəsˈfakSH(ə)n|

n. the triumph of being wronged by others

123

6
|siks|

RAGE

COMMISERATE + RAGE

COMMISERAGE

|kəˈmizərāj|

n. the disdain for those who don't share one's problems

THE THINGS THESE PEOPLE ARE CLAIMING WERE THEIR "BIGGEST LIFE OBSTACLES" AREN'T EVEN DIFFICULT THINGS. THEY'RE JUST REGULAR THINGS THAT HAPPEN TO EVERYONE ALL THE TIME.

LIKE, WHAT, YOU GOT APPENDICITIS WHEN YOU WERE 9 AND SPENT 3 DAYS IN THE HOSPITAL? TRY BEING DIAGNOSED WITH AN INCURABLE AUTOIMMUNE DISEASE WHEN YOU ARE 20 AND BEING SICK FOR THE REST OF YOUR LIFF, YOU DUMB B.

AW, A GUY BROKE UP WITH YOU IN A TEXT MESSAGE? TRY GETTING DUMPED BY YOUR CHEATING BOY-FRIEND ON YOUR 30TH BIRTHDAY WHILE IN PUERTO RICO FOR CHRISTMAS, AND THEN CRASHING A CAR AND GETTING STRANDED IN THE JUNGLE ALONE, AND ALSO YOU'RE TWO MONTHS SOBER. *WOOF.*

OH, POOR BABY, YOUR PARENTS GOT DIVORCED WHEN YOU WERE 6? TRY BEING 13 AND HAVING...

DUDE, YOU *HAVE* TO STOP WATCHING *THE BACHELOR.*

CONTROL + CONTEMPT

CONTREMPT

|kənˈtrempt|

n. the resentment of being the most responsible or
capable member of a group or relationship

STRESSFUL + LULL

STRULL

|strəl|

n. (between two or more persons) the escalating period of passive-aggressive tension that inevitably ends in a massive eruption

DISAGREEMENT + FRUSTRATION

DISAGRATION

|disəˈgrāSHən|

n. exasperation from never being on the same page as another person

SUBJECTIVITY + INDIGNATION
SUBJECTIGNATION

|səbˈjektəˈnāSHən|

n. the injustice of incongruous perspectives

VINDICATION + DESPERATION

VINDESPERATION

|vin͵despəˈrāSHən|

n. the immediate urge to redeem oneself after realizing what
one should have said or done a moment too late

DISAPPOINTED + INCREDULOUS
DISCREDULOUS

|disˈkrejələs|

adj. (of a person) shocked/confused by a loved one's failure to understand something valued

n. **DISCREDULITY**

WHEN MY BOYFRIEND CONFESSED HE DIDN'T LIKE THE MOVIE *CLUELESS*, I WAS SO DISCREDULOUS I BROKE UP WITH HIM.

PRE- + REJECTION

PREJECTION

|prē'jekSHən|

n. rejection from someone whom one was already planning on rejecting

135

ANGER + ANTHROPOMORPHIZE

ANGERPOMORPHIZE

|ˈaNGərpəˌmôrfīz|

v. to ascribe agency and/or ill will to inanimate objects

I STUBBED MY TOE ON THE COMPUTER CHARGER I HAD LEFT ON THE FLOOR, THREW IT ACROSS THE ROOM, AND SCREAMED, "WHY DOES EVERYTHING EXIST TO SPITE ME?"— ANGERPOMORPHIZING THE HELPLESS ELECTRONIC.

FLIGHT + FLATULENCE
FLIGHTULENCE

| ˈflīCHələns |

n. the bad gas one gets from the pressure changing in an airplane

SUPERIOR + SELF-CONGRATULATORY

SUPERIALATED

|sə͵pi(ə)rēəˈlātd|

adj. secretly feeling better than another after listening to them complain about doing something one has already done without complaint

VAPIDITY + FRUSTRATED

VAPIDATED

|ˈvapədādəd|

adj. exasperated from listening to people quibble over trivial things

139

SMACK + SMILE
SMACKLE

|smakəl|

v. to follow a vindictive statement with a sugary grin

THERE'S NOTHING MORE SATISFYING THAN WINNING AN ARGUMENT WITH A SPOT-ON DIG, A HAIR FLIP, AND A WELL-TIMED SMACKLE.

HOSTILITY + SOLIPSISM

HOSTILIPSISM

|ˌhəˈstälipsizm|

n. aggression toward others due to the inability to see outside oneself

IT'S IMPOSSIBLE TO TRY TO REASON WITH SOMEONE
WHO IS SO HOSTILIPSISTIC, EVERYTHING YOU SAY IS AN ATTACK,
AND BEFORE YOU'VE EVEN HAD A CHANCE TO RESPOND
SHE STORMS OUT WITH A CHEESY HAIR FLIP AND A SMACKLE.

HOSTILE + NOSTALGIA

HOSTALGIA

|həˈstaljə|

n. rage from the inability to retrieve the past

STRESS + CRUMBLE

STRUMBLE

| ˈstrəmbəl |

v. to deteriorate into nothingness from stress and exhaustion

7

|sevuhn|

FOR SHAME

INTRUDE + PHOBIA

INTRUDOPHOBIA

|inˈtroodəˈfōbēə|

n. the fear of burdening people with one's presence

INSECURITY + PROJECT

INSOJECT

|ˌinsəˈjekt|

v. to believe someone doesn't like you based
on no actual evidence suggesting so

DRAMATIC + DRASTIC

DRAMASTIC

|drəˈmastik|

adj. theatrical and exaggerated in one's reaction to any given situation, compounded by extremeness and often volatility

Submitted by Big-Time Feeler
Sam Lansky (@samlansky)

APOLOGETIC + VOLATILE
APOLOTILE

|əˈpälətl|

adj. embarrassed after overreacting or being impulsive

EMOTION + MODULATE

EMODULATE

|iˈmäjəˌlāt|

v. to temper one's true emotions around others

SOMETIMES WHEN I MEET SOMEONE FOR THE FIRST TIME, I TRY TO EMODULATE MYSELF, SO AS NOT TO ENCUMBER THEM WITH MY INTENSITY.

RELIVE + MORTIFICATION

REMORTIFICATION

|rē͟ˌmôrtəfəˈkāSHən|

n. the masochistic urge to recall memories
of shame and/or embarrassment

GUILT + INTROVERSION

GUILTROVERSION

|ˈgiltrəˌvərZHən|

n. the guilt from wanting to see no one and do nothing

153

PRODUCTIVE + PROCRASTINATE

PRODUCTINATE

|prəˈduktəˌnāt|

v. **1.** to work on a selfish endeavor in lieu of an obligatory assignment
2. to put off completing an obligatory assignment
by working on a selfish endeavor

FAUX + FOCUS

FAUXCUS

|ˈfōkəs|

v. to devote a great deal of time and effort to a pointless task

GRODY + SHOCK

GROCK

|gräk|

v. to shock oneself by one's own grodiness

I SPOTTED A GIRL ON THE OTHER SIDE OF A WINDOW AND THOUGHT, *YIKES! THAT GIRL NEEDS A SHOWER!* THEN I REMEMBERED, *OH WAIT, THAT'S A MIRROR! OH WAIT! THAT'S ME.* AND I WAS SO GROCKED I FAINTED.

EMOTION + PRIORITIZE
EMOTITIZE

|iˈmōdəˌtīz|

v. to prioritize emoting above all else (seeing friends, family, work, attending events or social gatherings) in one's life

PENITENT + NARCISSISM
PENISSISM

|ˈpenəˌsizm|

n. guilt from realizing one has been excessively self-involved

DELIBERATE + HATE

DELIBERHATE

|deˈlibərhāt|

v. to consciously choose anger over empathy for a person

SUBSTITUTE + ABSOLVE

SUBSOLVE

|səbˈzälv|

v. to clear one's own conscience at the expense of someone else's feelings

REMISS + MISTAKEN

REMISTAKEN

|remə'stāk ən|

adj. ashamed from realizing another was right about something one repeatedly defended one's position against

GUILT + RETRIBUTION

GUILTRIBUTION

|ˌgiltrə'byooSHən|

n. remorse from successfully actualizing revenge

FAMILY + DISCONNECTION
DISFAMILIATION

|ˌdisfəmiléˈāshən|

n. the guilt of not liking or relating to one's family

MAL- + CRAVE

MALCRAVE

|mal'krāv|

v. to desire something that is generally considered bad or taboo

8

|eyt|

FLEETING MOMENTS OF HAPPINESS

INCREDULOUS + ELATION

INCREDULATION

|inˌkrejəlāˈSHən|

n. the surprised excitement of having something go exceptionally well

FREEDOM + RELAPSE

FREELAPSE

|ˈfrēlaps|

n. to hook up with an ex with no emotional repercussions

PRODUCTIVITY + LIBERATION

PRODUCTERATION

|prə͵dəktərˈāSHən|

n. the satisfaction of crossing things off one's literal or figurative to-do list

CALAMITY + OPPORTUNITY

CALAMITUNITY

|kəˌlamˈt(y)oonədē|

n. the prevention of a potential disaster by discovering
an opportunity hidden in the crisis

n. an opportunity hidden in a crisis

CANCEL + ELATED
CANCELATED

|ˈkansəˌlātd|

adj. relieved about a dreaded plan falling through at the last minute

ROCK BOTTOM + METAMORPHOSIS

ROCK-BOTTOMORPHOSIS
(also, bottomorphosis)

|răkˌbätəˈmôrfəsəs|

n. (of a person) the transformation that occurs only from experiencing a self-loathing so strong one feels true desire to change

BLISSFUL + IGNORANT

BLIGNORANT

|ˈblignərənt|

adj. possessing a jolly naiveté about life and the world

MUSIC + NOSTALGIA

MUSTALGIA

|ˌmyoōzˈstaljə|

n. the visceral feeling that hearing a song from one's past evokes

EVOLVE + EPIPHANY

EVOLVEPIPHANY

|iˌvälviˈpifənē|

n. the realization of growth and improvement by doing something that once took much time and effort, but which one now does with great ease

UNPLANNED + TRANSFORMATION

UNPLANSFORMATION

|ənˌplansfərˈmāSHən|

v. to accidentally grow or change one's feeling about something by expressing false optimism about it

EPIPHANY + DESTINY

EPIPHESTANY

|epiˈfestənē|

n. the realization that all your problems are smaller than you think*

*Often due to gazing out at a vast space and realizing how large the earth is in comparison to how small you are

FRACTION + REALIZE

FRACTALIZE

| ˈfraktəlīz |

v. to realize everything in life is either a microcosm
or a macrocosm of everything else

PERFECT + CONFIDENCE
PERFIDENCE

|ˈpərfədns|

n. the feeling of something's unmistakable perfection or completeness

SOLITARY + CONTENT

SOLITENT

|ˈsälətənt|

adj. in a state of peaceful solitude

n. **SOLITENTMENT** |sälәˈtentmint| the comfort of being alone

DEFEATED + ILLUMINATED
DELLUMINATED

|di'loomə̩nātd|

adj. relieved from realizing a bleak truth

SOLACE + VALIDATION

SOLIDATION

|ˌsäləˈdāSHən|

n. the relief of feeling wholly understood by another

EMOTIONAL + REVELATION

EMOVELATION

|i͡ˌmōvəˈlāSHən|

n. the excited clarity one feels from learning a new word
that describes an emotion one didn't realize one felt

The End.

ACKNOWLEDGMENTS

Ben Schrank and everyone at Razorbill, who for some reason thought it was a good idea to let me make a book.

Jessica Almon, my editor, who somehow made sense of my pages of gibberish and brain vomit, and managed to make it look like I knew what I was doing. Without your notes, revisions, guidance, and endless patience, this book would have been nothing more than drivel on a Google doc.

Erin Malone, my agent, whose belief in me and this project is the only reason any of this was possible.

Samira Iravani and Theresa Evangelista, the brilliant designers who made this book beautiful. They made my words worth looking at, and, let's be real—they are the reason you picked up this book in the first place. (As *if* we don't all judge books by their covers.)

All the artists and friends and creative humans who helped me bring this thing to life when it was just a Twitter, then website, then rebooted website, then book proposal, etc.: Doug Bensimon, Emily Bernstein, Amy Bloom, Nate Bryson, Ryan Bundra, Sarah Chiarot, Grant Dickie, Rafe Goldberg, Elizabeth Graeber, Adam Griffin, Ally Kalt, Jason Katzenstein, Aditi Khorana, Hashtag David Lowe, Vivi Mildenberger, Serena Parr, Kit Rich, Emily-Anne Rigal, Sara Shillinglaw, Bill Skrzyniarz, Sharon Watts.

Charlie, for spending hours sitting with me in my trailer and convincing me my ideas were not garbage.

Sam, for talking me off all the ledges.

Sandy, my personal Yoda, the most beautiful angel of light and love, for your inspiration and optimism, for making me truly understand the concepts of gratitude and accepting myself, and for teaching me how to "release someone to their greatest and highest good," a mantra that I now recite ad nauseum.

My beautiful, loyal, loving friends—Katie Baker, Ally Conover, Vincent Covello, Dani Goodman, Rachel Keller, Abby Kramer, Kaitlin Magowan, Aly Monroe, Allyn Morse, Alison Quinn, Alex Reid, Zach Robinson, Daryl Sabara, Robin Shorr, Beth Soroko—for your relentless support and encouragement from the very beginning, for listening to my daily (read: hourly [read: minutely]) epiphanies about absolutely nothing, and for listening to me abuse the phrase "release them to their greatest and highest good" and still wanting to be my friends.

My mother, for having blind confidence in me always, who taught me there were "no mistakes in art," and who always made me believe I could do anything, even when we both knew I really couldn't. (I really couldn't play softball.)

My brothers, Cosmo and Ben, for putting up with me.

Cronny, for allowing me to "real quick get your opinion on this" at all hours of the day, real quick giving me your opinion on this at all hours of the day, letting me feel all the feelings at you, giving me attention and validation when I would plead for attention and validation, knowing when not to give me attention and validation when I would plead for attention and validation, playing me Beach Boys when I would sob on the floor for no reason, and, of course, giving me the inspiration for the word *unimflation*, you know-it-all dick.

And Julia, my illustrator extraordinaire, collaborator, Partner in Crime, Fairy-Godmother-Book-Guru-Therapist-Friend-Bombass-Comics-Maker. Thanks for having a telepathic way of understanding my nonsense ideas, always knowing exactly what I was asking for, even when I didn't. Thanks for not just bringing my words to life but for going above and beyond any sort of "illustrator duties," guiding me through every step of the book-making process, allowing me to ask all the stupid questions. Thanks for always shooting me straight, never hesitating to tell me when my ideas were stupid, boldly assuring me when they were good, and always bringing your own (usually better) ideas to the table. Thanks for responding to my fan e-mail three years ago, asking if you by any chance maybe might be interested in helping me with "this thing I'm trying to make." Thanks for taking my seedling of an idea and showing me how to make it an actual, real-life book. For you, I will never have the words to express my gratitude.

OFFICIAL
FEELINGS INDEX